Mission

Our mission is to provide independent, relevant, and timely oversight of the Department of Defense that supports the warfighter; promotes accountability, integrity, and efficiency; advises the Secretary of Defense and Congress; and informs the public.

Vision

Our vision is to be a model oversight organization in the Federal Government by leading change, speaking truth, and promoting excellence—a diverse organization, working together as one professional team, recognized as leaders in our field.

Objective

We determined whether DoD properly accounted for Force Provider (FP) equipment in Afghanistan. An FP module is a compilation of components that support 600 personnel.

Findings

The Army did not properly account for the 62 FP modules deployed to Afghanistan from 2001 through 2013, valued at approximately $424.57 million. This occurred because the Army did not verify that FP equipment was recorded on the receiving unit's accountability records and because the Deputy Chief of Staff of the Army, G-4 (DA G-4) did not require nonexpendable components to be tracked separately by serial number. As a result, the Army could not hold units responsible for proper use, care, and disposition of equipment deployed to Afghanistan, which included estimated losses of $200 million worth of FP equipment prior to 2010.

In addition, the Army did not require item managers to assign accurate and cost-effective accounting requirements codes (ARCs) to FP components. This occurred because DA G-4 published conflicting guidance and did not have a process in place to validate that item managers assigned accurate ARCs to FP equipment. As a result, item managers assigned

incorrect ARCs to 17 FP components, valued at $41.96 million, which increased the risk that the equipment would be lost, destroyed, or abandoned in theater.

Recommendations

Among other recommendations, we recommend that DA G-4 identify and account for all nonexpendable FP components by serial number and revise AR 735-5 to ensure items are correctly assigned accounting requirements codes.

We also recommend that the Commanding General, Army Materiel Command, establish guidance that lists the responsibilities regarding the accountability of FP equipment and require 401st AFSB to conduct quarterly reconciliations of property books to the equipment that has been deployed into theater.

Management Actions

The Chief of Staff, Regional Command South secured secret- and controlled-inventory items that we identified at Kandahar Air Field and opened an investigation on the abandoned equipment. Additionally, the Chief, DA G-4 Property Accountability Division and Defense Logistics Agency personnel confirmed that they changed 10 of the 17 miscoded ARCs. This effort ensured that the items would be handled in accordance with AR 735-5.

Management Comments and Our Response

The Deputy Chief of Staff of the Army, G-4 and Commanding General, Army Materiel Command, did not respond to the draft report. Therefore, we request that they provide comments in response to this report. Please see the Recommendations Table on the next page.

Recommendations Table

Management	Recommendations Requiring Comment	No Additional Comments Required
Deputy Chief of Staff of the Army, G-4	A.1. and B.1.	
Commanding General, Army Materiel Command	A.2.a., A.2.b., B.2.a., and B.2.b.	

Please provide comments by September 1, 2014.

July 31, 2014

MEMORANDUM FOR AUDITOR GENERAL, DEPARTMENT OF THE ARMY

SUBJECT: The Army Did Not Properly Account For and Manage Force Provider Equipment in Afghanistan (DODIG-2014-098)

We are providing this report for review and comment. The Army did not properly account for Force Provider modules deployed to Afghanistan from 2001 through 2013. Further, the Army did not ensure accurate accounting requirements codes were assigned to individual Force Provider components. This increased the risk that units would improperly destroy, abandon, or lose Force Provider equipment in theater, which could result in increased reset costs.

The Deputy Chief of Staff of the Army, G-4 and Commanding General, Army Materiel Command, did not respond to the draft report. DoD Directive 7650.3 requires that recommendations be resolved promptly. Therefore, we request comments on all recommendations in this report by September 1, 2014.

Please provide comments that conform to the requirements of DoD Directive 7650.3. Please send a PDF file containing your comments to audrco@dodig.mil. Copies of your comments must have the actual signature of the authorizing official for your organization. We cannot accept the / Signed/ symbol in place of the actual signature. If you arrange to send classified comments electronically, you must send them over the SECRET Internet Protocol Router Network (SIPRNET).

Comments provided on the report must be marked and portion-marked, as appropriate, in accordance with DoD Manual 5200.01. If you consider any matters to be exempt from public release, you should mark them clearly for Inspector General consideration.

We appreciate the courtesies extended to the staff. Please direct questions to me at (703) 604-8905 (DSN 664-8905). If you desire, we will provide a formal briefing on the results.

Amy J. Frontz
Principal Assistant Inspector General
for Auditing

Contents

Contents (cont'd)

Introduction

Objective

Our audit objective was to determine whether DoD properly accounted for Force Provider (FP) equipment in Afghanistan. See Appendix A for the Scope and Methodology and Appendix B for a list of prior audit coverage.

Background

FP equipment is the Army's premier life support base camp system that is a containerized and highly deployable "tent city." The FP concept began in 1991 as a result of inadequate living conditions for soldiers during Operations Desert Shield and Storm. FP modules consist of military and commercial equipment, which includes climate-controlled billeting, food preparation and dining facilities, hygiene services, and morale, welfare and recreation facilities. FP modules accommodate up to 600 personnel and can also be divided into four, 150-man expeditionary base camps. FP can be issued as a complete module or as individual expeditionary base camps. A single FP module is packaged in approximately 103 triple containers, five 20-foot containers, 27 trailer-mounted generators, and assorted other self-storing items. This facilitates transportation by any combination of air, rail, land, and sea. See Figure 1 below for examples of FP module setup in Afghanistan.

Figure 1: FP Triple Containers and Tents at Bagram Airfield, Afghanistan

FP is part of Army Prepositioned Stocks[1] (APS) and is recorded as Theater Provided Equipment[2] (TPE) when deployed. The Army produced five different versions[3] of FP modules: A, B, C, D, and E. The Army only deployed versions B, C, and D to Afghanistan and is only retrograding[4] items from versions C and D that TACOM Life Cycle Management Command (TACOM) identified as required for reset.[5]

Force Provider Roles and Responsibilities

Multiple commands, offices, and other organizations throughout the Army are involved in the deployment and retrograde of FP equipment. The most notable are the:

- Office of the Deputy Chief of Staff of the Army, G-4 Logistics (DA G-4) provides guidance on developing the APS program, which includes FP equipment prior to Afghanistan deployment. DA G-4 also issues the order to release the FP equipment from APS and directs Army Materiel Command (AMC) to ship FP equipment in support of the operational needs statement (ONS).[6]

- Army Sustainment Command (ASC), a subordinate command of AMC, manages the APS, including FP. In addition, ASC leverages a global network of Army Field Support Brigades (AFSB), logistics support teams, and brigade logistics support teams to provide materiel readiness visibility and management, including property accountability, depot reset induction and equipment redistribution. AMC tasks ASC to prepare FP equipment for transfer to the requesting unit.

- 401st AFSB, headquartered at Bagram Airfield, Afghanistan, a subordinate command of ASC, executes, directs, and manages field- and sustainment-level logistics for U.S. and selected coalition forces in Afghanistan. 401st AFSB provides ASC a forward presence by executing APS and the TPE programs.

---

[1] Assets that are strategically placed around the world to rapidly equip forces deploying to contingencies, stability, or support operations, or to enable realistic training exercises.

[2] Theater Provided Equipment is equipment that is received, drawn, or purchased in theater. Further, TPE is designated by the Army to remain in the Area of Responsibility for the duration of the mission.

[3] The Army refers to the different versions of FP modules as revisions; for simplification, we refer to them as versions throughout the report.

[4] The process for the movement of non-unit equipment and materiel from a forward location to a reset (replenishment, repair, or recapitalization) program or to another directed area of operations to replenish unit stocks, or to satisfy stock requirements.

[5] To restock equipment to a desired level of combat capability that meets a unit's future mission requirements.

[6] The ONS outlines and justifies the requesting units need for FP equipment.

AMC tasks ASC with ensuring that force provider equipment is transferred to the 401st AFSB's TPE records through the Army retail accountability system known as Property Book Unit Supply Enhanced (PBUSE). 401st AFSB also oversees the retrograde of TPE in Afghanistan.

- TACOM is a major subordinate command of AMC and consists of the following major organizations: PEO Ground Combat Systems; PEO Combat Service and Combat Service Support; PEO Soldier; Integrated Logistics Support Center; and Acquisition Center. Product Manager Force Sustainment Systems (PdM FSS), which is in PEO Combat Service and Combat Service Support, is the material developer and has total life cycle management responsibility for FP. The Soldier Product Support Integration Directorate, which is under the Integrated Logistics Support Center, provides total life cycle logistics and materiel readiness support and is the wholesale manager of FP. Based on direction from AMC, personnel in the Integrated Logistics Support Center provide a material release order[7] to 401st AFSB and then transfer the FP equipment to 401st AFSB or directly to deployed units. PdM FSS and the Soldier Product Integration Directorate maintain a presence in Afghanistan to support the identification and retrograde of FP equipment needed for reset. The Soldier Product Integration Directorate also oversees the 320 Yard[8] at Bagram Airfield.

For a full overview of individual roles and responsibilities of all organizations associated with the deployment and retrograde of FP, see Appendix C.

Deployment and Issuing Process

The flow chart in Figure 2 represents the Army's deployment and issuing process for FP equipment. The flowchart identifies areas where the Army could potentially lose accountability of FP equipment after the equipment is no longer tracked by the Army.

---

[7] A material release order is an order to release and transfer materiel.

[8] The 320 yard is a plot of land specifically designated by the Army to process FP equipment. It is used by TACOM and 401st AFSB for processing FP equipment for retrograde.

Figure 2: FP Equipment Deployment and Issuing Process

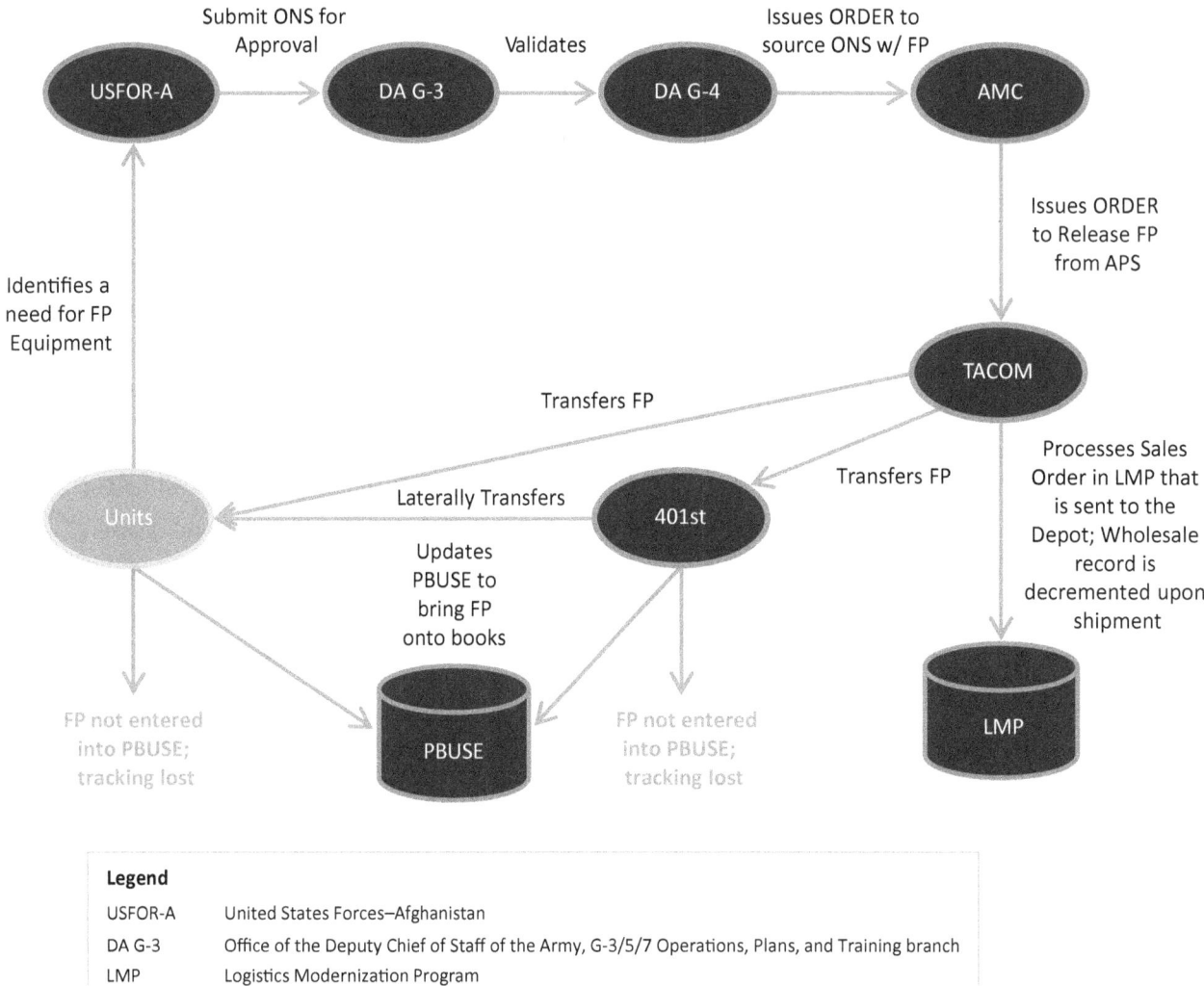

Retrograde Process

FP equipment that the Army tracked using PBUSE has a different process than the equipment that was not entered in PBUSE. FP equipment accounted for in PBUSE goes through the Redistribution Property Assistant Team yard and the formal TPE planner process for disposition and retrograde while FP equipment that was not accounted for in PBUSE goes through the retrosort yard[9] and 320 yard for disposition and retrograde. However, a unit could also send its FP equipment that was not in PBUSE directly to Defense Logistics Agency (DLA)–Disposition Services (DS) for destruction. See Figure 3 for the Army's process for the retrograde of FP equipment.

---

[9] The retrosort yard is an equipment turn in facility operated by the 1103rd Combat Sustainment Support Battalion. They are responsible for providing redistribution, retrograde, and disposal services for units across the Combined Joint Operations Area– Afghanistan in order to gain visibility and accountability of excess non-mission essential equipment and materiel that is not on property books.

Figure 3: FP Retrograde Process

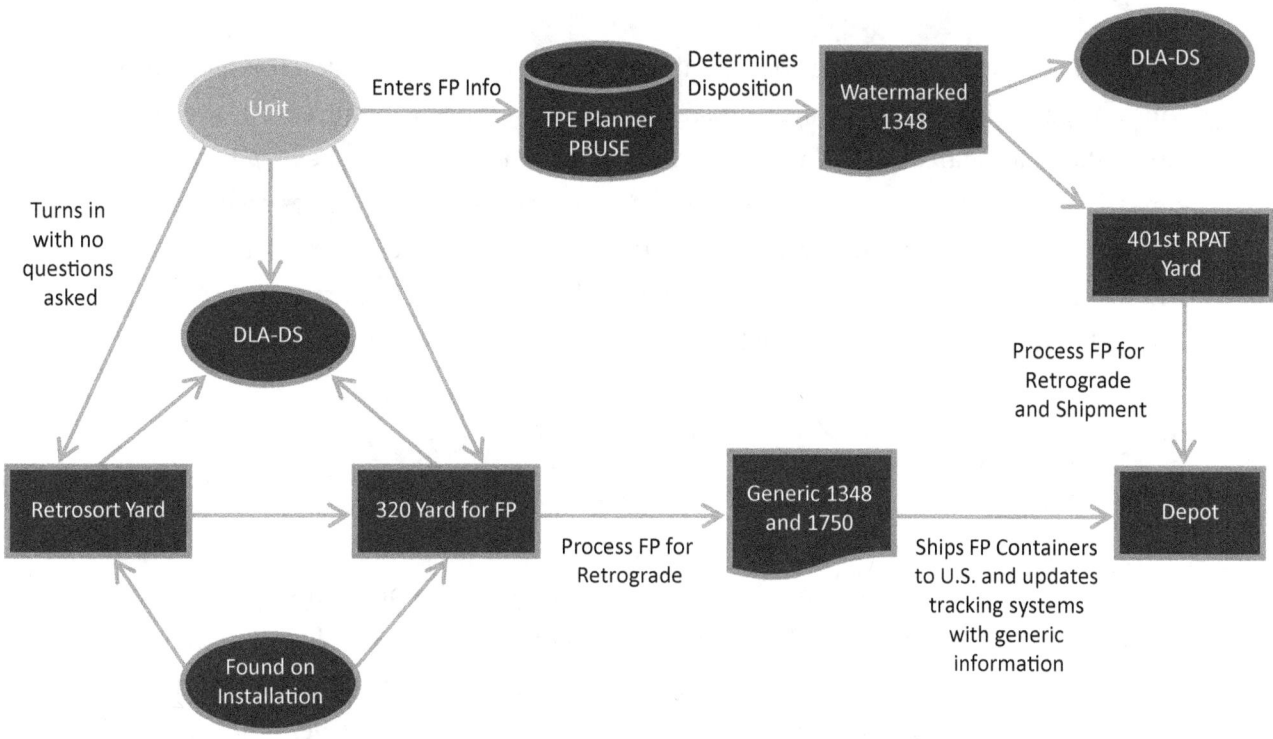

1. TPE Planner a web-based automation tool that assist units in determining the disposition of their TPE that is accounted for in PBUSE.
2. Watermarked 1348s are generated by TPE Planner only for FP equipment that was accounted for in PBUSE.
3. DLA-DS disposes of excess property in theater.
4. Redistribution Property Assistance Team Yard (RPAT Yard) is run by 401st AFSB and assists units by receiving, processing, and shipping equipment turned in by units, including TPE.

Army Accountability Requirements

There are several Army and DoD policies that describe how the Army should account for equipment. The most notable are Army Regulations (AR) 735-5, "Property Accountability Policies," August 22, 2013, and 710-2, "Inventory Management-Supply below the National Level," March 28, 2008. AR 735-5 provides guidance for accounting for Army property and accounting for lost, damaged, or destroyed Army property. It states that all property acquired by the Army from any source must be accounted for with continuous accounting from the time of acquisition until the ultimate consumption or disposal of the property occurs and that supporting documentation must be maintained. It further states that all Army property, except real property, is assigned an accounting requirements code (ARC) of expendable, durable, or nonexpendable. The ARC identifies the degree of accounting and control that must be applied at the user level. Nonexpendable property requires formal accountability throughout the life of the item. Nonexpendable items will be accounted for at the using-unit level using property book procedures in accordance with AR 710-2.

AR 710-2 provides guidance for the accountability and assignment of responsibility for property issued to a unit. It states that all property acquired by the Army, regardless of source, needs to be accounted for, and that all nonexpendable items must be accounted for on a formal property book.[10] It further states that property book records must provide a complete trail (suitable for audit) for all transactions. In addition, all employees of the Army, both military and civilian, are required to turn in all found Government property to the supply system for disposition.

Review of Internal Controls

DoD Instruction 5010.40, "Managers' Internal Control Program Procedures," May 30, 2013, requires DoD organizations to implement a comprehensive system of internal controls that provides reasonable assurance that programs are operating as intended and to evaluate the effectiveness of the controls. We identified internal control weaknesses in the accountability of FP equipment in Afghanistan. Specifically, the Army did not properly account for the 62 FP module equivalents deployed to Afghanistan from 2001 through 2013, valued at approximately $424.57 million. In addition, the Army did not properly manage FP components in the version C and D FP modules deployed to Afghanistan. We will provide a copy of this report to the senior official responsible for internal controls in the Department of the Army.

---

[10] Organizations and activities using an automated property book accounting system are not required to keep manual records that duplicate information available from the automated system (such as the property book document register and due-in suspense file). All property book records must provide a complete trail (suitable for audit) for all transactions.

Finding A

The Army Needs to Improve Accountability of Force Provider Equipment

The Army did not properly account for the 62 FP module equivalents[11] deployed to Afghanistan from 2001 through 2013, valued at approximately $424.57 million. Specifically:

- Army did not account for 43.25 FP module equivalents, valued at $284.64 million. This occurred because the Army did not verify that FP equipment was recorded on the receiving unit's accountability records.

- Although ASC and 401st AFSB recorded 18.75 FP module equivalents, valued at $139.93 million, DA G-4 did not require ASC and 401st AFSB to track the modules at a level that would allow for adequate accountability if deployed units separated components from the module. This occurred because DA G-4 procedures for tracking FP equipment were not consistent with AR 710-02 policy for accounting for nonexpendable[12] property.

As a result of the Army's lack of accountability of FP equipment, the Army could not hold units responsible for proper use, care, and disposition of equipment deployed to Afghanistan. This increased the risk that units would improperly destroy, abandon, or lose FP equipment in theater, ultimately resulting in increased reset costs. Since $284.64 million worth of FP equipment was never accounted for, the Army could not determine how much FP equipment was improperly destroyed, lost or abandoned. However, TACOM personnel estimated that the Army generated a loss of $200 million worth of FP equipment prior to 2010 due to poor accountability, and we found $287,860 worth of FP equipment abandoned during site visits to two bases in Afghanistan.

---

[11] One FP module can be separated into four expeditionary base camps. As a result, one expeditionary base camp equals 0.25 of an FP module equivalent.

[12] Nonexpendable property is not consumed in use and retains its original identity during the period of use. Nonexpendable property requires formal property book accounting after being issued to the user level.

The Army Did Not Record FP Equipment in the Accountability System

The Army did not account for 43.25 FP module equivalents deployed to Afghanistan, valued at $284.64 million, in PBUSE. Prior to 2006, the Army did not have an adequate process to ensure units brought the equipment to record after it was transferred to the unit from the Logistics Civil Augmentation Plan vendor. However, even after a process for recording FP property as TPE was developed, ASC and 401st AFSB still did not verify that FP equipment was properly recorded in the unit's account in PBUSE, the Army's retail accountability system, after it was removed from the wholesale[13] accountability system, referred to as LMP.[14]

The Army Did Not Account for All Deployed FP Modules

The Army did not account for 43.25 FP module equivalents deployed to Afghanistan. In total the Army deployed 62 FP modules valued at $424.57 million to Afghanistan from 2001 through 2013. The DA G-4 attempted to identify and obtain full accountability of FP equipment in Afghanistan in August of 2010. Specifically, DA G-4 issued a memorandum to the Commanding General, U.S. Army Central Command requiring units to establish formal property accountability of all FP modules and add-on kits in Southwest Asia. The Army deployed 48.25 FP module equivalents to Afghanistan from 2001 to 2010; however, 401st AFSB only accounted for 2 of those 48.25 FP module equivalents in PBUSE prior to the memorandum. The Army deployed an additional 13.75 FP module equivalents to Afghanistan from 2010 through 2013. However despite the memorandum, the Army still only accounted for 18.75 FP module equivalents valued at $139.93 million in PBUSE as illustrated in table 1.

> The Army did not account for 43.25 FP module equivalents deployed to Afghanistan.

---

[13] Wholesale items are generally stored in distribution warehouses, sometimes called inventory control points, where they are held pending requisitions from the retail supply system. As the retail system requires parts, it requisitions the needed items from the wholesale supply system.

[14] LMP is the Army's Enterprise Resource Planning system used to record Army logistical and financial transactions.

Table 1: FP Equipment Not Historically Accounted for in Theater (as of January 2014)

FP Description	Quantity of FP Module Equivalents Deployed	Quantity of FP Module Equivalents in PBUSE	Value in PBUSE (millions)	Quantity of FP Module Equivalents Not in PBUSE	Value not in PBUSE (millions)
Version B (Light)	16	3	$18.90	13	$81.90
Version B	21	2	$12.66	19	$120.27
Expeditionary Base Camp	6	1.75	$11.20	4.25	$27.20
Version C	7	3	$22.88	4	$30.50
Version D	12	9	$74.29	3	$24.76
Total	**62**	**18.75**	**$139.93**	**43.25**	**$284.64***

*Total does not equal the actual sum due to rounding.

AR 735-5 requires that all property acquired by the Army from any source must be continuously accounted for from the time of acquisition until the ultimate consumption or disposal of the property occurs and that supporting documentation be maintained. However, the Army did not maintain continuous accountability of 43.25 FP module equivalents, valued at $284.64 million that the Army deployed to Afghanistan since 2001.

The Army Did Not Properly Transfer Accountability to Deployed Units

The Army did not maintain continuous accountability of FP modules deployed to Afghanistan since 2001. Originally, the Army used the Logistics Civil Augmentation Plan vendor to transfer equipment to the units. However, the Army did not have an adequate process prior to 2006 to ensure units brought the equipment to record once it was transferred from the vendor, thus losing accountability of the FP equipment sent to Afghanistan.

In 2006, the Army established a process to record and track FP equipment as TPE. This process should have ensured that the FP equipment accountability was transferred to deployed units. Despite this new process, the Army did not maintain continuous accountability of FP modules deployed to Afghanistan. Specifically, ASC and 401st AFSB did not verify that FP equipment was recorded on the receiving unit's accountability records as TPE. ASC and 401st AFSB attributed the loss of accountability to multiple reasons. According to 401st AFSB personnel the DA product managers were responsible for ensuring that the receiving unit accounted for the FP equipment in PBUSE as TPE. Additionally, the 401st AFSB stated they received a surge of FP equipment in 2009 and, at that time, FP accountability was not a top priority. Furthermore, ASC personnel stated that 401st AFSB was not responsible for recording FP equipment in PBUSE until DA G-4 officially issued a memorandum in August 2010. However, ASC and 401st AFSB personnel should have ensured that incoming FP equipment was recorded in PBUSE as TPE.

> The 401st AFSB stated they received a surge of FP equipment in 2009 and, at that time, FP accountability was not a top priority.

Since August 2006, DA G-4 orders, which authorized the release of FP equipment, have stated that FP equipment should be added as TPE to the theater property book. As the forward presence of ASC, 401st AFSB maintains theater-wide asset visibility of all TPE and accountability of all equipment designated as TPE. It is the theater property book officer's responsibility to transfer accountability of the FP equipment to the requesting unit. In addition, ASC is responsible for accounting for, issuing, and transferring accountability of APS equipment, including FP, to deploying units. However, ASC and 401st AFSB personnel did not always ensure incoming FP equipment was recorded in PBUSE.

Equipment Transfer Process Lacked Accountability

There is no clear guidance that specifies how FP equipment should be transferred from LMP to PBUSE or identifies the individuals involved in the process. The Army needs to issue FP-specific guidance that ensures that it is continuously accounted for from deployment to retrograde. Additionally, AMC should emphasize the importance of supply discipline and accountability to ensure complete property accountability for future contingency operations where FP is deployed. The Commanding General, AMC should establish clear guidance that details ASC and 401st AFSB's responsibilities regarding the accountability of FP equipment in theater. The guidance should specify which command is responsible for executing the transfers of accountability that are associated with the deployment, issuance, and retrograde of FP equipment. In addition, AMC should require the 401st AFSB theater property book officer to conduct quarterly reviews to validate the FP equipment that is recorded in the PBUSE system to the FP equipment that has been deployed to that theater.

FP Equipment Not Tracked at Adequate Level

DA G-4 did not require ASC and 401st AFSB to adequately track FP module equivalents that were accounted for in PBUSE. Specifically, DA G-4 only required ASC and the

401st AFSB to track FP modules in PBUSE using a national stock number (NSN)[15] and line-item number (LIN)[16] rather than by the nonexpendable components that compose the modules. Each FP module contains over 28,000 components of which approximately 548 are nonexpendable. Table 2 shows the separate LIN and NSN combinations that DA G-4 used to track the 62 FP modules deployed to Afghanistan. As illustrated, the Army used only one LIN (F28973) to track eight versions of the FP modules and two LINs (EB1901 and EB1902) to track the two versions of Expeditionary Base Camps that were deployed to Afghanistan. Furthermore, since LINs are not unique to the equipment, there is not sufficient information to identify which modules are recorded in the accountability system because the modules are not tracked by serial number.

Table 2: List of LINs and NSNs for FP Modules

Nomenclature	LIN	NSN	Quantity Deployed	Quantity Brought to PBUSE Record
Expeditionary [v. D] (Green)	F28973	5419-01-566-1156	0	0
Expeditionary [v. D] (Tan)	F28973	5419-01-566-1160	12	9
Expeditionary, Heavy [v. C] (Green)	F28973	5419-01-571-6445	2	2
Expeditionary, Heavy [v. C] (Tan)	F28973	5419-01-571-6447	5	1
Module [v. B] (Green)	F28973	5419-01-439-7807	0	0
Module [v. B] (Tan)	F28973	5419-01-399-6391	2	1
Module Lite [v. B] (Green)	F28973	5419-01-473-2294	19	1
Module Lite [v. B] (Tan)	F28973	5419-01-473-2297	16	3
Expeditionary Base Camp (Green)	EB1901 EB1902	5419-01-548-5063	3	.25
Expeditionary Base Camp (Tan)	EB1901 EB1902	5419-01-548-5064	3	1.50
Total			62	18.75

---

[15] The 13-digit stock number consisting of the 4-digit federal supply classification code and the 9-digit national item identification number.

[16] A LIN is a number assigned to a generic item description that identifies the line on which the generic item description is listed.

Modules Were Separated From Original Configuration

ASC and 401st AFSB risked losing accountability of the 18.75 FP module equivalents, valued at $139.93 million, which it accounted for in PBUSE after the FP modules were separated from their original configuration. In addition to the 18.75 FP module equivalents, 401st AFSB tracked 682 components, valued at $28.91 million, separately in PBUSE. 401st AFSB and TACOM personnel stated that it is common for units in Afghanistan to separate components from their original module. For example, a commander might decide to transfer a portion of an FP module, such as an expeditionary base camp, latrine, shower, or laundry, to another base, separating the FP module from its original configuration.

However, because the Army is only accounting for FP modules at the modular level rather than by the nonexpendable components contained in each module, it was not possible to determine if the proper transfer of accountability always occurred. In addition, we could not determine which of the 62 FP modules the 682 components originally belonged. Finally, because units separated FP modules in the field without 401st AFSB's knowledge, we could not determine if FP components were counted more than once or if all separated FP components were accounted for by the units in PBUSE.

> It was not possible to determine if the proper transfer of accountability always occurred.

DA G-4 Needs Greater Visibility of FP Components

The DA G-4 did not follow requirements in AR 710-02 when establishing procedures for accounting for FP equipment in PBUSE. Specifically, AR 710-02 requires that all property acquired by the Army, regardless of source, needs to be accounted for and that all nonexpendable items are required to be recorded in a formal property book after issued to the user. Tracking FP components at a modular level does not meet the intent of AR 710-02 because it combines over 500 nonexpendable items into one line in PBUSE. When only the LIN and NSN are used to track the FP module, the nonexpendable components are not adequately tracked. This creates severe accountability challenges for FP modules when nonexpendable components are separated from their original configuration, which according to 401st AFSB and TACOM personnel happens often. As a result, we could not determine whether the modules recorded in PBUSE were complete. Specifically, nonexpendable components could have been separated from the original configuration, and the current process for FP accounting would not have identified this action in PBUSE.

Many of the nonexpendable items that compose a module were given a serial number before being deployed. However, DA G-4 did not require this information to be captured by ASC and 401st AFSB in PBUSE. If the Army uses serial numbers and NSNs, it could track most nonexpendable components on current and future versions to prevent the loss of accountability and visibility when FP modules are separated from their original configuration. The Deputy Chief of Staff of the Army, G-4 should identify and account for all nonexpendable Force Provider components by serial number in the Army accountability systems to maximize accountability and visibility of FP equipment when deployed.

Lack of Accountability Increased the Risk of Improper Disposition

The Army could not hold units responsible for proper use, care, and disposition of FP equipment deployed to Afghanistan because they did not fully account for FP equipment. For example, TACOM personnel identified 47 FP components that they determined were cost effective to retrograde out of Afghanistan for the reset of future modules (see Appendix D). However, the Army mismanaged these items, which increased the risk that units would improperly destroy, abandon, or lose FP equipment in theater. This ultimately would result in increased reset costs.

> The Army could not hold units responsible for proper use, care, and disposition of FP equipment deployed to Afghanistan.

Poor Accountability May Have Resulted in Improper Destruction

The Army's poor accountability increased the risk that DLA-DS would unknowingly destroy FP items that TACOM desired for reset. As of February 2014, DLA-DS processed $23.14 million worth of FP equipment. Of that amount, $6.97 million worth of FP equipment was in serviceable or repairable condition, $641,811 of which TACOM desired for reset. However, the data obtained from DLA-DS may not have included all the FP equipment turned in for disposal. Specifically, DoD Office of the Inspector General Report No. DODIG-2014-007, "Defense Logistics Agency Disposition Services Afghanistan Disposal Process Needed Improvement," November 8, 2013, stated that the DLA-DS records were not always accurate or complete. Further, FP equipment that units coded as unserviceable could have been serviceable. Specifically, TACOM personnel stated that condition codes were not always accurate because sometimes units assigned equipment unserviceable-condemned-condition codes to "get the property off their hands so they can redeploy."

The unit turning the equipment into DLA-DS is supposed to be the technical expert on the property requiring disposal. Therefore, other than ensuring the equipment received for disposal is accurately listed on the turn-in document, DLA-DS personnel are not required to validate the accuracy of anything else on the turn-in document, including the condition code. DLA-DS personnel also are not required to assess if there was a need for the equipment in theater or if the item should be retrograded. Instead, DLA-DS relied on the unit to make those determinations, and the units were not always reliable. For example, there was an instance in 2010 when DLA-DS notified TACOM personnel prior to processing the equipment that 18 FP generators and 19 environment control units, valued at approximately $789,267, were dropped off at DLA-DS. The equipment was nearly new and should not have been destroyed. TACOM personnel recovered some of the equipment in this instance, but there was no way to hold anyone accountable. TACOM personnel stated that this occurrence initiated an aggressive patrolling of DLA-DS sites, which resulted in TACOM personnel recovering numerous FP items that were improperly turned in.

The Amount of Equipment Lost or Abandoned Was Unknown

401st AFSB could not determine the amount of FP equipment lost or abandoned in Afghanistan because the Army did not maintain continuous accountability of $284.64 million worth of FP equipment. From 2011 through 2013, 401st AFSB reported $7.77 million worth of FP equipment losses on their Financial Liability Investigation of Property Loss tracker.[17] However, the amount of FP items listed on the tracker did not accurately represent the amount of FP equipment lost in Afghanistan because it did not capture FP equipment not accounted for in PBUSE or lost prior to 2011. For example, TACOM personnel estimated that prior to 2010 the Army generated a loss of more than $200 million in FP equipment due to poor accountability.

Further, without proper accountability, the risk of units abandoning equipment significantly increases. For example, we identified two instances of abandoned FP equipment at two bases in Afghanistan where we conducted fieldwork. At Bagram Airfield, we identified approximately $183,860 worth of FP equipment that a unit had abandoned in a yard for at least 7 months. At Kandahar Airfield, we identified at least $104,000 worth of FP equipment in an abandoned yard that had been left unsecured and exposed to the elements for an unknown amount of time. Figure 4 provides an example of discarded FP inventory we observed at the abandoned yard at Kandahar.

---

[17] Financial Liability Investigations of Property Loss support the voucher used to adjusts the accountability records when Government property has been lost or damaged.

Figure 4: FP Kitchen Container Full of Equipment Abandoned on Kandahar Airfield, Afghanistan

In addition to the FP equipment at Kandahar, we identified secret- and controlled-inventory items in open containers and triwalls in the same unsecured yard. We communicated our observations to retrosort yard officials at Kandahar and Regional Command South personnel for immediate attention. The Chief of Staff Regional Command South immediately secured the secret- and controlled-inventory items and opened a security investigation to determine how the items were abandoned at the lot. The Regional Command South investigation determined that the yard contained a total in excess of 1,874 items, valued at over $2.2 million, including 28 sensitive items valued over $380,000 and 2 high-dollar items valued over $442,000. The investigation concluded that due to systemic failures in the property accountability procedures, the investigators could not determine with definitive accuracy any individual that could be held liable for the abandoned items.

Lack of Accountability Will Increase Reset Costs

Reset costs increase when units improperly destroy, lose, or abandon FP equipment. According to Program Executive Office Combat Support and Combat Service Support personnel, it costs an average of $4.3 million[18] to reset an FP module versus $12.8 million to purchase a new module. These amounts included the costs of retrograding equipment. Therefore, in order to bring a module back to fully mission capable status, the Army would need to repurchase items that units improperly destroyed, lost, or abandoned in Afghanistan at a much greater price than if the equipment had been properly retrograded.

Conclusion

The Army needs to improve its accountability of deployed FP equipment. The Army did not account for 43.25 FP module equivalents, valued at $284.64 million, out of the 62 FP module equivalents that were deployed to Afghanistan. In addition, the Army tracked 18.75 FP module equivalents, valued at $139.93 million, but it did not account for the equipment at a level that allowed adequate accountability. The Army could make improvements by tracking nonexpendable components by serial number and by establishing clear guidance on who is responsible for accounting for FP equipment when deployed.

Recommendations

Recommendation A.1

We recommend that the Deputy Chief of Staff of the Army, G-4 identify and account for all nonexpendable Force Provider components by serial number in the Army accountability systems.

---

[18] This amount does not include replacement for any major end items either not returned from theater, beyond economical repair, or replaced due to a configuration change.

Recommendation A.2

We recommend that the Commanding General, Army Materiel Command:

a. Establish clear guidance that details the Army Sustainment Command's and 401st Army Field Support Brigade's responsibilities for accountability of Force Provider equipment in theater. The guidance should specify which command is responsible for executing the transfers of accountability that are associated with the deployment, issuance, and retrograde of Force Provider equipment.

b. Require the 401st Army Field Support Brigade theater property book officer to conduct quarterly reconciliations of the Force Provider equipment that is recorded in the Property Book Unit Supply Enhanced system to the Force Provider equipment that has been deployed to that theater.

Management Comments Required

The Deputy Chief of Staff of the Army, G-4 and the Commanding General, Army Materiel Command, did not provide comments on the draft report. We request that the Deputy Chief of Staff of the Army, G-4 and Commanding General, Army Materiel Command, provide comments on the final report.

Finding B

The Army Did Not Properly Manage Force Provider Components

The Army did not properly manage FP components in the version C and D FP modules[19] deployed to Afghanistan. Specifically, the Army did not require FP item managers to assign accurate and cost-effective ARCs, which prescribe how units should account for Army equipment. This occurred because DA G-4:

- published conflicting guidance in AR 735-5 that assigned all class IX[20] FP equipment as expendable ARCs regardless of the cost or characteristics of the item; and

- did not have a process in place to validate that item managers assigned accurate ARCs to class II FP equipment.

As a result, item managers inaccurately assigned expendable ARCs to 17 FP components, valued at $41.96 million. Consequently, units were not required to account for the 17 FP components even though the equipment should have been assigned nonexpendable or durable ARCs, which require formal property book accounting or hand receipt controls. In addition, since expendable property is not required to be turned in by the units, while nonexpendable and durable equipment should be turned in, this deficiency also increased the risk that the incorrectly coded FP equipment would be lost, destroyed, or abandoned in theater.

---

[19] Of the 62 FP module equivalents deployed to Afghanistan, 25 were versions C and D. The remaining 37 FP module equivalents were version B, which PM FSS and TACOM personnel did not want for reset. Therefore, we did not review the ARCs for those 37 FP module equivalents.

[20] The Army divides all of its supplies into 10 classes. An FP module is composed of class II, class VII, and class IX components. Class II includes individual equipment, tents, and organizational tool sets and kits; class VII equipment consist of major end items, such as kitchens and showers; and class IX includes repair parts and components, such as assemblies and subassemblies.

ARCs Determine How the Army Will Account for Equipment

ARCs determine how items are accounted for in an Army accountability system. Specifically, based on guidance prescribed in AR 735-5, all Army property is assigned an ARC, which classifies property as nonexpendable, durable, or expendable.

- **Nonexpendable** property is not consumed in use and retains its original identity during the period of use. Nonexpendable property requires formal property book accounting throughout the life of the item and is required to be turned in for retrograde.

- **Durable** property is not consumed in use and does not require formal property book accounting but, because of its unique characteristics, requires other property accountability controls when issued to the user. AR 735-5 further states that personal property having a unit cost between $500 and $5,000, and not otherwise coded nonexpendable, is durable. Durable equipment should be required to be turned in for retrograde.

- **Expendable** property is consumed in use, loses its identity in use, or has a unit cost of less than $500. The Army does not require any formal property book accounting after issue to the user level and it is not required to be turned in for retrograde.

Item Managers Assign ARCs to Equipment

Item managers are responsible for assigning ARCs to the equipment they procure and manage. The U.S. Army Soldier's Biological and Chemical Command was responsible for purchasing and managing the FP components, such as the kitchens and showers. As such, the Army assigns the corresponding ARCs to those items. However, DLA also buys several FP components, and is assigned as the item manager for these components. DLA personnel stated that several years ago, the Logistics Support Activity, a subordinate command of the Army Materiel Command, instructed DLA to code all DLA-managed equipment as expendable. As a result, all items purchased by DLA are managed and accounted for as if they were consumed in use regardless of the ARC that AR 735-5 prescribed the item should receive. DLA personnel stated that if the Army would like DLA to assign a nonexpendable or durable ARC to an item it manages, it is the Army's responsibility to contact DLA to arrange for the item to be recoded.

The Army Should Assign Cost-Effective ARCs to Class IX Components

The Army did not require item managers to assign accurate and cost-effective ARCs to class IX FP components in the version C and D FP modules that were deployed to Afghanistan. Specifically, all class IX FP components were managed as expendable regardless of the characteristics of the item. For example, one of the class IX FP components, an electrical power distribution box, was coded as expendable despite having a unit cost of $8,107.52 and a total value of $210,795.52 for the 26 distribution boxes that were required to reset an entire module. (See Appendix E for a listing of the seven class IX components.) This occurred because DA G-4, as the proponent of AR 735-5, developed and published conflicting guidance that stated all class IX equipment should be assigned expendable ARCs, no matter the cost or any other characteristics of the item.

> The Army did not require item managers to assign accurate and cost-effective ARCs to class IX FP components.

As a result, DLA assigned expendable ARCs to seven class IX components, totaling $13.14 million, which should have been coded as nonexpendable or durable. Specifically, none of the seven class IX items were consumed in use, lost their identity in use, or had a unit cost of less than $500, but they were coded as expendable because AR 735-5 stated that all class IX items should be labeled as such. In addition, TACOM identified all seven class IX items as cost effective to retrograde from Afghanistan, further demonstrating that the items would not be consumed in use and should have been properly accounted for. By publishing guidance that required item managers to assign expendable ARCs to all class IX items, DA G-4 did not require units to formally account for or turn in the FP equipment for retrograde, which increased the risk that the Army would not get the equipment back.

To ensure item managers assign Army equipment the most accurate and cost-effective ARCs regardless of the class of the equipment, the Deputy Chief of Staff of the Army, G-4 should revise AR 735-5 to ensure items that are not consumed in use, do not lose their identity in use, and have a unit cost of more than $500 are assigned nonexpendable or durable ARCs.

The Army Did Not Assign Accurate ARCs to Class II Components

The Army did not properly manage 10 class II FP components in the version C and D FP modules that were deployed to Afghanistan. Specifically, the Army did not require item managers to assign ARCs in accordance with AR 735-5. AR 735-5 prescribed which Army supply classes should be assigned nonexpendable, durable, and expendable ARCs. For supply classes that are not explicitly referenced in AR 735-5, the guidance provides a dollar-value range for determining the ARC of an item. However, AR 735-5 was not being used when assigning ARCs to DLA-managed items. Specifically, if an FP item was managed by DLA, it would be assigned an expendable ARC no matter what the supply class or dollar value of an FP component was. DLA officials stated that this deficiency originated because the Logistics Support Activity made the decision to code all DLA-managed items as expendable. However, the problem persisted and was unresolved for several years because DA G-4, who is ultimately responsible for the equipment, did not have a process in place to validate that the item managers assigned accurate ARCs to the FP equipment they managed.

As a result, DLA assigned expendable ARCs to 10 class II FP components, valued at $28.81 million, that AR 735-5 stated should have been coded nonexpendable or durable. AR 735-5 stated that all Army equipment with an 8340 federal supply code that is an end item should be coded with a nonexpendable ARC and all equipment with a 7340 federal supply code be coded with a durable ARC. However, 9 FP end items with Federal Supply Codes of 8340 and one FP item with a 7105 code were all coded as expendable. Expendable equipment is managed as if it was consumed upon issuance and requires no accountability, while nonexpendable requires formal property book accountability and durable equipment requires hand receipt controls. In addition, expendable equipment is not required to be turned in for retrograde. Incorrectly assigning expendable ARCs to the 10 FP components meant that units could dispose of the equipment, which increased the risks that the Army would not get the equipment back. (See Appendix F for a listing of the items that DLA incorrectly coded.)

> DLA assigned expendable ARCs to 10 class II FP components, valued at $28.81 million, that AR 735-5 stated should have been coded nonexpendable or durable.

Actions Taken to Address Incorrect ARCs

On January 10, 2014, we informed the Chief, DA G-4 Property Accountability Division of our concerns that FP components were miscoded with inaccurate ARCs. The chief subsequently communicated with DLA personnel, and on January 30, 2014, DLA personnel confirmed that they had submitted cataloging actions to recode the 10 ARCs from expendable to nonexpendable. We determined that the efforts taken by DA G-4 and DLA ensured the items would be handled in accordance with AR 735-5. Specifically, because DLA changed the ARCs for the 10 class II FP items from expendable to nonexpendable, the Army now requires units to maintain FP equipment using formal property accounting. In addition, units are responsible for turning the 10 items in for retrograde and are responsible for lost equipment. As a result, DA G-4 and DLA have decreased the risk that units will improperly lose, destroy, or abandon the 10 FP components.

Although DA G-4 addressed this deficiency for FP, DLA is the item manager for a significant amount of Army equipment. Consequently, this other Army equipment may have been assigned incorrect ARCs. In addition, DLA may not be the only item manager that Army officials instructed to code items as expendable. The Commanding General, AMC, should conduct a review to determine whether all Army equipment has been assigned ARCs that are in accordance with the revised AR 735-5. This should include requiring that all item managers assign the most accurate ARCs according to AR 735-5. Once AMC has conducted this review and has ensured item managers are coding Army equipment in accordance with AR 735-5, the Commanding General AMC should develop a process for periodically validating whether the item managers assigned ARCs that were in accordance with the revised AR 735-5.

Conclusion

The Army needs to improve its accountability of FP equipment. The Army allowed DLA to code 17 FP components, valued at $41.96 million, with ARCs that were not accurate and cost-effective. Specifically, units were not required to account for or maintain FP equipment using formal property accounting procedures, and the Army could not hold the units accountable for the loss of the FP equipment. The Army could improve the accountability of FP equipment by clarifying AR 735-5 to identify items that should be coded as nonexpendable more effectively and by reviewing all FP equipment to determine if item managers assigned accurate and cost effective ARCs.

Recommendations

Recommendation B.1

We recommend that the Deputy Chief of Staff of the Army, G-4 revise AR 735-5, "Property Accountability Policies," to ensure items that are not consumed in use, do not lose their identity in use, and have a unit cost of more than $500 are assigned nonexpendable or durable accounting requirement codes.

Recommendations B.2

We recommend the Commanding General, Army Materiel Command:

    a. Conduct a review to determine whether all Army equipment has been assigned accounting requirement codes that are in accordance with the revised Army Regulation 735-5 , "Property Accountability Policies,"

    b. Develop a process for periodically validating whether the item managers assigned accounting requirement codes that were in accordance with the revised Army Regulation 735-5, "Property Accountability Policies."

Management Comments Required

The Deputy Chief of Staff of the Army, G-4 and the Commanding General, Army Materiel Command, did not provide comments on the draft report. We request that the Deputy Chief of Staff of the Army, G-4 and Commanding General, Army Materiel Command, provide comments on the final report.

Appendix A

Scope and Methodology

We conducted this performance audit from October 2013 through June 2014 in accordance with generally accepted government auditing standards. Those standards require that we plan and perform the audit to obtain sufficient, appropriate evidence to provide a reasonable basis for our findings and conclusions based on our audit objectives. We believe that the evidence obtained provides a reasonable basis for our findings and conclusions based on our audit objective.

We reviewed DoD and Army criteria to gain an understanding of the regulations for the accountability of Force Provider equipment in Afghanistan. Specifically, we reviewed the Quartermaster Force Provider Company Field Manual No. 4-20.07, 401st AFSB Property Accountability: Internal Standard Operation Procedures, AR 710-1, "Centralized Inventory management of the Army Supply System," AR 710-2, "Inventory Management – Supply below the National Level," AR 735-5, "Property Accountability Policies," DoD Instruction 5000.64, and "Accountability and Management of DoD Equipment and Other Accountable Property."

We reviewed and documented the deployment and issuance process for FP equipment in Afghanistan. To accomplish this, we relied on meetings held with DA G4, 401st AFSB, TACOM, PdM FSS, and contractors who processed FP equipment. We also reviewed operational needs statements, operations orders, and other orders that facilitated the deployment of FP equipment into Afghanistan. From this information, we created a deployment process flowchart. We also obtained and analyzed Commodity Command Standard System and LMP data queries from TACOM and combined them with release orders from DA G-4 to determine the quantity, type, and value of FP modules deployed to Afghanistan. We also compared the Material Release Orders, Commodity Command Standard System, and LMP with the transaction history in PBUSE to determine the number for FP module equivalents that 401st AFSB accounted for in PBUSE and the number of FP modules equivalents not accounted for in PBUSE.

Additionally, we determined whether DLA assigned the correct ARC for FP equipment that TACOM identified as desired for reset. We used the TACOM provided disposition instructions for version C and version D to identify what TACOM required and desired for reset. We then reviewed Force Provider catalogs and used Logistics Information Warehouse to identify the ARCs assigned to the FP equipment required and desired for reset. We reviewed Army Regulations 735-5, "Property Accountability Policies" and 710-2, "Inventory Management – Supply Below the National Level" to understand the guidance pertaining to ARCs. Using the guidance in AR 735-5 and AR 710-2, we independently determined what the ARC should be for the FP equipment required and desired for reset. Then, we created a spreadsheet of the required and desired FP items that included their currently assigned ARCs and what their ARCs should be based on the disposition instructions.

We also assessed the amount of FP equipment that had been disposed of or reported lost on a Financial Liability Investigation of Property Loss. We met with DLA-DS, TACOM, and 227th Quartermaster Company and reviewed DLA-DS guidance to determine the process and procedures in place for the transferring of accountability of FP equipment to DLA-DS and its disposal of that equipment. We used a DLA-DS provided data query to determine the amount and condition of FP equipment that has been processed by DLA-DS since 2002. Further, we reviewed the 401st AFSB TPE Financial Liability Investigation of Property Loss tracker to determine the quantity, type, and value of FP equipment lost and documented on a Financial Liability Investigation of Property Loss from 2011 through 2013.

We reviewed and documented the Army's retrograde process of FP equipment in Afghanistan. To accomplish this, we interviewed personnel from TACOM, 401st AFSB, U.S. Transportation Command, Letterkenny Army Depot, and contractors who processed FP equipment. We obtained retrograde data provided by Program Executive Office Combat Support and Combat Service Support, PM FSS, TACOM, and 401st AFSB to understand the Army's retrograde process, estimates, and tracking systems. We created a retrograde flowchart using this information. We developed a spreadsheet that analyzed a 401st AFSB provided Army War Reserve Deployment System data pull of retrograded equipment to determine the quantity, type, and value of retrograded FP equipment.

On December 7, 2013, the audit team notified the Regional Command officials of unsecured secret and sensitive items located in an abandoned yard in Kandahar Airfield. We discovered the unsecured secret and sensitive equipment while searching for FP equipment. We inventoried select items at the yard, ranging from large machinery and FP equipment to high end military electronic devices of classified and sensitive nature. To inventory the items, we used a camera to take pictures of the item as well as any identifiable information such as part number, serial number, NSN, and Commercial and Government Entity codes. Using Web Federal Logistics Information Service, we entered an item's identifiable code into the system to generate the item's pertinent information such as NSN, cost, and controlled inventory item code. We reviewed and cited the various Army Regulations that the unsecured secret and sensitive items violated. To follow-up the audit team visited Regional Command South headquarters to ensure the secret and sensitive items had been secured.

Use of Computer-Processed Data

We received computer-processed data from LMP, Commodity Command Standard System, PBUSE, 401st AFSB TPE Financial Liability Investigation of Property Loss Tracker, and Distribution Supply System to determine whether the Army maintained proper accountability of FP equipment during the deployment, issuance, and retrograde or disposal of the equipment in Afghanistan. LMP, Commodity Command Standard System, PBUSE, the TPE Financial Liability Investigation of Property Loss Tracker, and Distribution Supply System are used by the Army to maintain accountability and visibility over wholesale and retail assets from its purchase to disposition.

We did not rely on the Financial Liability Investigation of Property Loss Tracker or Distribution Supply System as primary support for our conclusions. Therefore, we did not evaluate the sufficiency or reliability of the data within these systems. To verify the reliability of the data in LMP and Commodity Command Standard System, we tested transactions by comparing them to supporting documentation provided by DA G-4 and TACOM. From these procedures, we determined that the documentation in LMP and Commodity Command Standard System was incomplete, but was sufficiently reliable when combined together for the purpose of acquiring deployment data for our analysis. We focused our analysis on whether the Army adequately accounted for FP equipment in PBUSE by comparing the deployment data for FP equipment to the FP equipment listed in the PBUSE historical record. The data reliability weaknesses we identified with PBUSE are discussed in the findings. We believe the computer processed data we used were sufficiently reliable to support the findings and conclusions in this report.

Use of Technical Assistance

The audit team met with members of the DoD IG Quantitative Methods Division to discuss selecting a sample of FP equipment and how to test it. The discussion included the possibilities of statistical testing. It was determined that any type of statistical testing would not be feasible.

Appendix B

Prior Audit Coverage

During the last 5 years, the Government Accountability Office (GAO), the Department of Defense Inspector General (DoD IG), and Army Audit Agency issued 10 reports discussing Government Property Accountability and equipment retrograde in Southwest Asia. Unrestricted GAO reports can be accessed over the Internet at http://www.gao.gov. Unrestricted DoD IG reports can be accessed at http://www.dodig.mil/pubs/index.cfm. Unrestricted Army reports can be accessed at https://www.aaa.army.mil/.

GAO

GAO-13-185R, "Afghanistan Drawdown Preparations: DoD Decision Makers Need Additional Analyses to Determine Costs and Benefits of Returning Excess Equipment," December 19, 2012

GAO-11-774, "Iraq Drawdown: Opportunities Exist to Improve Equipment Visibility, Contract Demobilization, and Clarity of Post-2011 DoD Role," September 16, 2011

DoD IG

DoD IG Report No. DODIG-2014-043, "The Army Needs to Improve Property Accountability and Contractor oversight at Redistribution Property Assistance Team Yards in Afghanistan" March 4, 2014

DoD IG Report No. DODIG-2014-007, "Defense Logistics Agency Disposition Services Afghanistan Disposal Process Needed Improvement," November 8, 2013

DoD IG Report No. DODIG-2012-138, "Wholesale Accountability Procedures Need Improvement for the Redistribution Property Assistance Team Operations," September 26, 2012

DoD IG Report No. DODIG-2012-071, "DoD's Management of the Redistribution Property Assistance Team Operations in Kuwait," April 10, 2012

Army

Army Audit Agency Report A-2013-0056-MTE, "Retrograde Sort Process, Afghanistan," February 26, 2013

Army Audit Agency Report A-2013-0048-MTE, "Materiel Management – Retrograde From Southwest Asia," February 1, 2013

Army Audit Agency Report A-2011-0077-ALL, "Follow-up of Retrograde Operations in Iraq-Class VII Theater Provided Equipment," April 12, 2011

Army Audit Agency Report A-2011-0063-ALL, "Redistribution Property Assistance Teams, United States Forces - Iraq," February 14, 2011

Appendix C

Roles and Responsibilities

United States Forces–Afghanistan

USFOR-A is a functioning command and control headquarters for U.S. forces operating in Afghanistan. The USFOR-A develops and submits the operational needs statement for the requesting unit to DA G-3 for approval.

Office of the Deputy Chief of Staff of the Army, G-3/5/7 Operation, Plans, and Training

The Office of the Deputy Chief of Staff of the Army, DA G-3 contributes to the success of APS by designing APS force structure that is compatible with the structure of the type of unit which will deploy to use APS equipment. DA G-3 validates the operational need statement from the requesting unit and approves the release of APS, including FP.

Office of the Deputy Chief of Staff of the Army, G-4 Logistics

DA G-4 provides guidance on developing the APS program, which includes FP equipment. DA G-4 ensures that APS materiel is combat ready for deploying units in accordance with Army serviceability standards. DA G-4 also ensures that APSs are kept at authorized levels to adequately fill unit sets; provides resources to conduct the APS program; approves listing of equipment to be included in APS; and ensures APS equipment requirements are identified in Army force structure, systems and applicable documents. After the operational needs statement is validated by the DA G-3, the DA G-4 issues the order to release the FP equipment from APS. The DA G-4 directs AMC to ship FP equipment in support of the operational needs statement. DA G-4 also determined the number of FP modules that the Army will reset to fill APS.

Army Materiel Command

AMC, headquartered at Redstone Arsenal, Alabama, is the Army's primary provider of material readiness, technology, acquisition support, material development, logistics power projection, and sustainment. AMC operates and maintains the APSs, including FP, and the Army's depots, including those storing and resetting FP equipment. The AMC issues the operation orders to release the FP equipment from the depots into Afghanistan.

Army Sustainment Command

ASC, headquartered at Rock Island Arsenal, Illinois, is the U.S. Army's logistics integrator for contingency and sustainment support for American fighting forces worldwide. ASC manages the APS, including FP, for AMC. In addition, ASC leverages a global network of Army field support brigades and battalions, logistics support teams, and brigade logistics support teams to provide materiel readiness visibility and management, including property accountability, depot reset induction and equipment redistribution. AMC tasks the ASC to prepare FP equipment for transfer to the requesting unit.

401st Army Field Support Brigade

401st AFSB, headquartered at Bagram Airfield, Afghanistan, executes, directs and manages field and sustainment level logistics for U.S. and selected coalition forces in Afghanistan. 401st AFSB command and controls two Army Field Support Battalions:

- the 3-401st Army Field Support Battalion, located at Bagram Airfield, Afghanistan, which supports regional commands east and north; and

- the 4-401st Army Field Support Battalion, located at Kandahar Air Field, Afghanistan, supports regional commands south and west.

401st AFSB provides ASC a forward presence by executing the APS and the TPE programs. The Army considers FP equipment to be TPE once it is deployed to Afghanistan. AMC tasks ASC with ensuring that force provider equipment is transferred to 401st AFSB's TPE records through their retail accountability system, PBUSE. 401st AFSB is also overseeing the retrograde of TPE in Afghanistan.

TACOM Life Cycle Management Command

TACOM, a major subordinate command of AMC headquartered in Warren, Michigan, unites all of the organizations that focus on soldier and ground systems throughout the entire life cycle. TACOM's mission is to develop, acquire, field, and sustain soldier and ground systems for America's warfighters. TACOM provides the material release order to one of the 401st Army Field Support Battalions located in Afghanistan. TACOM will either ship FP equipment to one of the 401st Army Field Support Battalions or directly to the units.

Letterkenny Army Depot

Letterkenny Army Depot (under the AMC chain of command) is headquartered in Chambersburg, Pennsylvania and is responsible for producing and resetting FP modules. According to TACOM officials the Army sends FP equipment retrograded from Afghanistan to the Letterkenny Army Depot to assist in the reset of FP modules.

Sierra Army Depot

The Sierra Army Depot in Herlong, California, which is managed by TACOM, is among the U.S. locations supporting the shipment of Force Provider. Operational Project Stocks material are stored and maintained at the depot.

Deployed Units

Deployed units in Afghanistan maintained and accepted accountability of FP equipment through PBUSE, when FP equipment was deployed to Afghanistan. The units should perform a full inventory of FP equipment when FP equipment is transferred to another unit during unit rotations. Finally, the unit uses TPE planner in PBUSE to determine the disposition of their FP equipment during retrograde if the FP equipment was accounted for in PBUSE.

Appendix D

Components Identified for Retrograde and Reset

The table below lists the FP items TACOM personnel identified as cost effective to retrograde out of Afghanistan for the reset of future modules.

NSN	Nomenclature	Quantity Required for Reset per Module	ARC	Unit Price	Total Cost per Module
5419015714107	Expeditionary Tricon Kitchen System, Green	4	N	$ 93,405.07	$ 373,620.28
4930016143654	Fuel Distribution System, Improved	4	N	$ 11,000.00	$ 44,000.00
6115014620291	Generator Set, 60kw, Mep 806b	26	N	$ 25,073.00	$ 651,898.00
5419015397178	Latrine System, Expeditionary, Green	8	N	$ 50,000.00	$ 400,000.00
5419015397180	Laundry, Containerized, Batch, Expeditionary, Green	4	N	$ 70,779.46	$ 283,117.84
5419015515432	Refrigerated Container, Tricon, Green	4	N	$ 19,949.00	$ 79,796.00
4630015138155	Waste Water Evacuation Tank/ Trailer	2	N	$ 49,465.00	$ 98,930.00
4520015666669	Heater, Water, Awh-400	4	N	$ 23,882.00	$ 95,528.00
5419015397182	Shower System, Expeditionary, Green	8	N	$ 50,000.00	$ 400,000.00
5419015430158	Shower Water Reuse System, Green	4	N	$ 125,000.00	$ 500,000.00
6150014701916	Distributing System, Outlet Assembly, Convenience, Temper, 3 Drop	96	X	$ 568.18	$ 54,545.28
8340015755528	As 10 Inch Airbeam Assembly	10	X	$ 1,721.93	$ 17,219.30
8340015754842	As End Section Liner, Iso End	4	X	$ 153.29	$ 613.16

NSN	Nomenclature	Quantity Required for Reset per Module	ARC	Unit Price	Total Cost per Module
8340015750614	As End Section Liner, Tricon	2	X	$ 153.29	$ 306.58
8340015753625	As End Section, Iso End, Green	4	X	$ 658.43	$ 2,633.72
8340015750619	As End Section, Tricon, Green	2	X	$ 652.87	$ 1,305.74
7105015522705	Bed, Bunk System W/ Fabric Trunklockers	320	X	$ 913.00	$ 292,160.00
6150012205588	Cable Assembly, Power, 60 Amp, 100 Ft Long	96	X	$ 985.43	$ 94,601.28
6150002558313	Cable Assembly, Power, 60 Amp, 50 Ft Long	56	X	$ 572.27	$ 32,047.12
6150012566304	Cable Assembly, Service, 100A, 50 Ft Long	28	X	$ 3,220.00	$ 90,160.00
A001-05-0058	Compressor, Air, Diesel, 17 Cfm	8	X	$ 480.46	$ 3,843.68
8145014154113	Container, Reusable, Bulk Equipment, Small	2	X	$ 1,155.50	$ 2,311.00
8150015287531	Container, Shipping And Storage-Triple (Tricon) With Connectors, Green	43	N	$ 4,523.00	$ 194,489.00
6110015547406	Electrical Power Distribution Box	26	X	$ 8,107.52	$ 210,795.52
4120016171273	Environmental Control Unit, F100-60	56	N	$ 17,787.00	$ 996,072.00
4320015806934	Pump Assembly, Containerized Shower	16	N	$ 4,552.00	$ 72,832.00
8145015034404	Shelf, Shipping And Storage	78	X	$ 44.33	$ 3,457.74
9540014913804	Shoring Beam	160	X	$ 62.96	$ 10,073.60
8340015593852	Tent, Temper Air Supported Structure, Type XXXI, 32 Ft, Green	36	X	$ 20,407.33	$ 734,663.88

NSN	Nomenclature	Quantity Required for Reset per Module	ARC	Unit Price	Total Cost per Module
8340015588698	Tent, Temper Air Supported Structure, Type XXXIV, 32 Ft, Green	4	X	$ 21,381.53	$ 85,526.12
8340015588701	Tent, Temper Air Supported Structure, Type XXXVII, 32 Ft, Green	4	X	$ 22,089.00	$ 88,356.00
8340015588703	Tent, Temper Air Supported Structure, Type XXXVIII, 21 Ft, Green	8	X	$ 18,705.56	$ 149,644.48
5180014830249	Tool Kit, General Mechanics	4	N	$ 1,805.00	$ 7,220.00
6110012510402	Temper Electrical Distribution Box, Type III, 120v	52	X	$ 1,702.77	$ 88,544.04
5419015714108	Expeditionary Tricon Kitchen System, Tan	4	N	$ 93,405.07	$ 373,620.28
5419015397179	Latrine System, Expeditionary, Tan	8	N	$ 50,000.00	$ 400,000.00
5419015397181	Laundry, Containerized, Batch, Expeditionary, Tan	4	N	$ 70,779.46	$ 283,117.84
5419015515431	Refrigerated Container, Tricon, Tan	4	N	$ 19,949.00	$ 79,796.00
5419015397183	Shower System, Expeditionary, Tan	8	N	$ 50,000.00	$ 400,000.00
5419015469681	Shower Water Reuse System	4	N	$ 125,000.00	$ 500,000.00
8340015750631	As End Section, Iso End, Tan	4	X	$ 658.43	$ 2,633.72
8340015750628	As End Section, Tricon, Tan	2	X	$ 652.87	$ 1,305.74
4120016171282	Environmental Control Unit, F100-60	56	N	$ 17,787.00	$ 996,072.00
8340015584701	Tent, Temper Air Supported Structure, Type XXXI, 32 Ft, Tan	36	X	$ 20,407.33	$ 734,663.88

NSN	Nomenclature	Quantity Required for Reset per Module	ARC	Unit Price	Total Cost per Module
8340015584699	Tent, Temper Air Supported Structure, Type XXXIV, 32 Ft, Tan	4	X	$ 21,381.53	$ 85,526.12
8340015584702	Tent, Temper Air Supported Structure, Type XXXVII, 32 Ft, Tan	4	X	$ 22,089.00	$ 88,356.00
8340015584703	Tent, Temper Air Supported Structure, Type XXXVIII, 21 Ft, Tan	8	X	$ 18,705.56	$ 149,644.48

Legend
(X) Expendable
(N) Nonexpendable

Appendix E

Components the Army Should Recode

The table below illustrates the 7 FP components that the Army should recode in the Version C and D FP modules to maximize accountability and recoverability of the items.

Item	Versions/ Colors that Included Item	Original ARC	Quantity Required for Reset per Module	Unit Price	Total Costs Per Module
Distributing System, Outlet Assembly	C and D (T&G)	X	96	$568.18	$54,545.28
60 AMP Power Cable Assembly, 100 Foot	C and D (T&G)	X	96	$985.43	$94,601.28
60 AMP Power Cable Assembly, 50 Foot	C and D (T&G)	X	56	$572.27	$32,047.12
100 AMP Service Cable Assembly, 50 Foot	C and D (T&G)	X	28	$3,220.00	$90,160.00
Reusable Bulk Equipment Container	D (T&G)	X	2	$1,155.50	$2,311.00
Electrical Power Distribution Box	C and D (T&G)	X	26	$8,107.52	$210,795.52
120V Electrical Distribution Box	D (T&G)	X	52	$1,702.77	$88,544.04

Legend
(G) Green FP module
(T) Tan FP module
(X) Expendable

Appendix F

Components Recoded by the Army

The table below illustrates the 10 FP components that the Army incorrectly coded in the version C and D FP modules.

Item	Versions/ Colors that Include Item	Original ARC	Correct ARC	Quantity Required for Reset per Module	Unit Price	Total Costs Per Module
Bunk Bed System	D (T&G)	X	D	320	$913.00	$292,160.00
Tent, Type XXXI, 32 Foot, Green	C and D (G)	X	N	36	$20,407.33	$734,663.88
Tent, Type XXXIV, 32 Foot, Green	C and D (G)	X	N	4	$21,381.53	$85,526.12
Tent, Type XXXVII, 32 Foot, Green	D (G)	X	N	4	$22,089.00	$88,356.00
Tent, Type XXXVIII, 21 Foot, Green	C and D (G)	X	N	8	$18,705.56	$149,644.48
Tent Liner, Type XXXVIII, Type C, Green	D (G)	X	N	2	$4,196.02	$8,392.04
Tent, Type XXXI, 32 Foot, Tan	C and D (T)	X	N	36	$20,407.33	$734,663.88
Tent, Type XXXIV, 32 Foot, Tan	C and D (T)	X	N	4	$21,381.53	$85,526.12
Tent, Type XXXVII, 32 Foot, Tan	D (T)	X	N	4	$22,089.00	$88,356.00
Tent, Type XXXVIII, 21 Foot, Tan	C and D (T)	X	N	8	$18,705.56	$149,644.48

Legend
(G) Green FP module
(T) Tan FP module
(X) Expendable
(D) Durable
(N) Nonexpendable

Acronyms and Abbreviations

AFSB	Army Field Support Brigade
AMC	Army Materiel Command
APS	Army Prepositioned Stocks
AR	Army Regulation
ARC	Accounting Requirements Code
ASC	Army Sustainment Command
DA G-3	Office of the Deputy Chief of Staff of the Army, G-3/5/7 Operations, Plans, and Training branch
DA G-4	Office of the Deputy Chief of Staff of the Army, G-4 Logistics
DLA	Defense Logistics Agency
DLA-DS	Defense Logistics Agency–Disposition Service
FP	Force Provider
LIN	Line Item Number
LMP	Logistics Modernization Program
NSN	National Stock Number
ONS	Operational Needs Statement
PBUSE	Property Book Unit Enhanced
PdM FSS	Product Manager Force Sustainment Systems
TACOM	TACOM Lifecycle Management Command
TPE	Theater Provided Equipment
USFOR-A	United States Forces–Afghanistan

Whistleblower Protection
U.S. Department of Defense

The Whistleblower Protection Enhancement Act of 2012 requires the Inspector General to designate a Whistleblower Protection Ombudsman to educate agency employees about prohibitions on retaliation, and rights and remedies against retaliation for protected disclosures. The designated ombudsman is the DoD Hotline Director. For more information on your rights and remedies against retaliation, visit www.dodig.mil/programs/whistleblower.